Backyard Naturalist

A Compilation of Nature Writing & Illustration

Carol Coogan

Backyard Naturalist
A Compilation of Nature Writing & Illustration.
Copyright © 2006-2007 by Carol Coogan.

To order additional copies of this title, contact your local bookstore.
The author may be contacted at the following address:
Carol Coogan
PO Box 3103
Albany, NY 12203

Cover and Book Design by: Carol Coogan
Illustrations by: Carol Coogan
www.carolcoogandesign.com

Printed by The Troy Book Makers in Troy, NY
on recycled, acid-free paper.
www.thetroybookmakers.com

ISBN-13: 978-1-933994-28-4
ISBN-10: 1-933994-28-2

Backyard Naturalist

A Compilation of Nature Writing & Illustration

Carol Coogan

VOLUME I

*Nature as observed in upstate New York's Capital Region
July 2006 through July 2007*

*This book is dedicated to the many readers of my
Times Union newspaper column, the "Backyard Naturalist,"
to fellow nature lovers, "I fish therefore I am,"
and to my best friend, Jayne.*

Contents

Forward

Famous naturalists of the 19th and early 20th centuries went into the field with writing and drawing implements, a sketchbook that often doubled as a notebook, and a walking stick for physical stability and protection. Maybe a backpack was also carried with binoculars, a hand lens and extra supplies. Today, a canteen of water may be added.

In the 1960's, when I was a student in Zoology at Syracuse University, we were required to take field notes and illustrate them. This was also true in laboratory classes such as parasitology and protozoology, where we were graded on the artistry and accuracy of the drawings and notes we kept on 3"x5" index cards for each species identified. Drawings meant close observation, and with notes, were likely to give one a better long term memory of the species or event. This is incredibly important when you want to quickly recall this information in the future, years or even decades ahead, to strengthen and back up one's memory.

Carol Coogan carries on this tradition. With sketches and notes, one can emphasize particular anatomic structures, behaviors and events that a camera cannot. Sketches and notes makes for a great combination, as is illustrated by Carol's Times Union "Backyard Naturalist" column, and subsequently in this book. Carol's artistry and insight into both common and uncommon plants, animals, and biological phenomena are unique, and her work is well worth pondering, while at the same time it is so enjoyable to look at. Everyone, including students in biology, amateur naturalists, as well as professional biologists, can pick up pointers from Carol's work that will make their observations more productive, and their memories of what they observed clearer and more interesting.

As people spend less time outdoors and interacting with nature, we know less about what our very survival is dependent upon. Following Carol's methods of nature study can bring you, your children, and even your grandchildren, more enjoyment and understanding of the wild. Going outside is good for the "soul," as well as the intellect, and there still is so much beauty and mystery to see and hear and experience out there, as I have long noted every day — and it's free. Whether you are rich or poor, you can always gain from nature.

Dr. Ward B. Stone, B.A., M.S., Sc. D. (Hon.)

Wildlife Pathologist, NYS Dept. Environmental Conservation
Adjunct Professor, SUNY Cobleskill
Adjunct Professor, College of Saint Rose

Introduction

Throughout my childhood, while others may have been playing with dolls, or setting up pretend tea parties, I was outside looking at spider webs, digging through dirt, or building secret forts behind the garage where I would quietly watch birds and squirrels undetected. I liked to sit under the lilac bushes, near where the raspberries and lilies-of-the-valley grew, and to this day I can easily recall the sweet aroma of flowers and earth. When indoors, I preferred nature documentaries over cartoons, and I was always reading, writing, drawing or passionately immersed in some sort of creative endeavor or another. I have never strayed far from those activities.

In the early eighties, I read Clare Walker Leslie's book, "The Art of Field Sketching," and was inspired to start a nature journal of my own, which I have kept — off and on — ever since. This eventually led to the creation of my weekly newspaper column, the "Backyard Naturalist." This book is a direct result of the requests from readers' of that column to have a compilation of my work published and made available to them.

I want to make a point to tell you that the style, usage and appearance of a nature journal is as vast and as varied as the many individual interests, backgrounds, education levels and motivations of the human populace. One person's journal may focus on prose and poetry, another's on scientific study, another's on list making with pasted in magazine photos, and yet another's on sketching and painting, or even a combination of all of these activities. Most of my journal entries are not polished and finished drawings, but are as rudimentary as a stick figure, or as haphazard and scratchy as an inexperienced scrawl, or may simply involve taping a leaf to the page.

What I remember most from my childhood was the freedom to explore, and that nature was everywhere for me to do just that. You don't need to travel to remote corners of the globe to learn about an amazing array of wildlife, flora and habitat. You can find it right in your own neighborhood, regardless of whether it be a small patch of weeds or acres worth of land. All it takes is curiosity and a few moments to observe and wonder, and you're on your way towards your own journey. It is my hope that my enthusiasm for nature will inspire you to begin an adventure of your own, or at the very least, that you will take time to consider the earth's beauty, intricacy and ingenuity, and become aware of the visceral connection we all have in common with the natural world around us.

Backyard Naturalist ————————— Carol Coogan

Wildflowers

Are you someone with a desire to observe, protect and understand the natural world? You could be a backyard naturalist. You don't need to travel to remote corners of the globe to learn about an amazing array of wildlife, flora and habitat. There's plenty to study in your own neighborhood.

Start with a curiosity about the natural world. Create a habit of careful observation. Somehow document what you notice and learn. For me, this takes the form of a nature journal. Begin exactly where you are. Walk outside, watch, listen, smell, touch, take notes, photographs, or make sketches.

Along a roadside, I note an abundant array of colorful beauty in the wildflowers growing there. What many call weeds have an unknown purpose, and play an intricate role in the balance of life. I hear a bird. I turn over a rock to watch what scurries away. Spying an entrance hole in an old wood chip pile, I wonder who lives there? Then I sketch. This is how one begins.

Albany South End
Warm, sunny, breezy

Red-tailed Hawk

Bumble Bee

Birdsfoot trefoil
(yellow)

Queen Ann's Lace

House Sparrow

House Mouse

Chicory
(blue)

Garden Centipede

July 2006

Black-eyed
Susan
(yellow-orange)

Mockingbird

Twice this week, I heard bird songs of such beauty and vocal virtuosity that I stopped in my tracks to listen. On both accounts, the culprit was a Northern Mockingbird.

Mockingbirds have an ability to mimic and assimilate such sounds as the songs of other birds, crickets, frogs, dogs, chimes and even squeaky gates into their own extraordinary song repertoire.

Their scientific name, Mimus polyglottos, means "many-tongued mimic." Before capturing and selling wild birds became illegal, the popularity of keeping Mockingbirds as caged pets nearly caused their extinction.

To attract a female mate in the spring, a male Mockingbird perches on an exposed, elevated area and sings loudly, then somersaults or leaps into circling loops of flight, only to return again to his perch to repeat the process. This continues all day, and sometimes all night, until a female arrives. If there is no success, most males eventually give up and move on. But a few will persistently continue singing and vaulting themselves into the air well into the midsummer season.

1pm
July 2006
Very hot day!
Corner of office building
in downtown Albany

Erie Blvd.

Leaps into the air. Flies around in loops.

Perched on top of a phone pole on the corner of Wolf Rd & Central

Beautiful singing!

Northern Mockingbird

Cicada

The sound of a Cicada, also known as the Dogday Harvestfly, is a sign of the summer season. It's rare that you'll actually see one. But around mid-afternoon on a hot summer day in July, when a loud, high pitched buzzing sound pierces the air and drones on like an electric saw, you'll know they're there.

Male Cicadas sit high in the treetops as they vibrate voice boxes on their abdomen, bouncing the sound off an internal amplifier to call for females. They are the loudest insects on earth.

Cicada's have an unusual life cycle. Eggs are laid in tree crevices. When they reach nymph stage, they fall, burrow underground, and feed on root sap for 2 to 5 years. Then one day, in the middle of the night, they crawl out of the dirt and attach to trees. Their skins split and shed. They emerge, inflate, and dry their wings to molt into adult Cicadas. Some Cicada species remain underground for 13 to 17 years before they emerge.

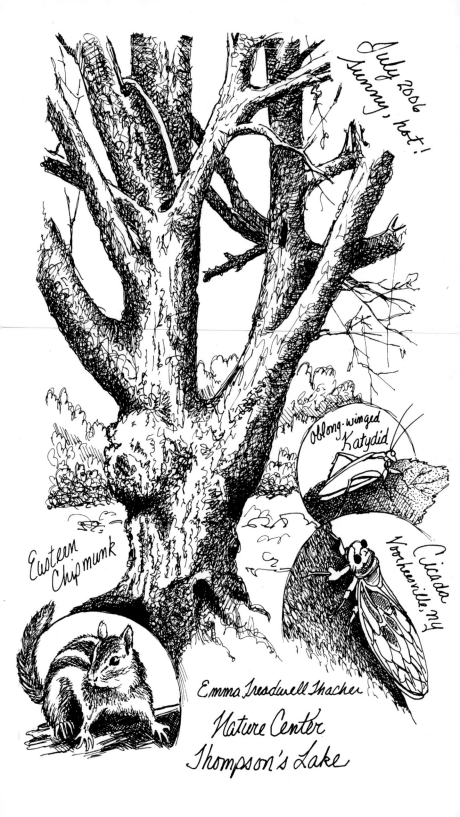

Great Blue Heron

It is an unforgettable and majestic sight to see a Great Blue Heron flying, head tucked back, long legs dangling behind, slowly beating its wings like some ancient Pterodactyl. Easily identified by their large size and unmistakable shape, they can reach a height of four feet, with a wingspan of up to six feet.

Great Blue Herons reside in wetlands along rivers, lakes and ponds, nesting in large colonies high in the treetops near their feeding grounds. I recently spotted a group of them resting along the Hudson River shoreline during a Dutch Apple cruise, long-legged, gray-blue silhouettes, standing hunched, motionless and silent at sunset.

I also observed them roosting and hunting along the Normanskill Creek. A Great Blue Heron stands very still in shallow water, stalking or waiting for its prey to come within striking distance. Folding its long, flexible neck back, poised, it then suddenly plunges headfirst into the water to grab and swallow its feast. Great Blue Herons primarily eat fish, frogs, snakes, water insects, voles and mice.

July
August
2006

Groups of
young herons
along the Hudson River

Great Blue Heron

Herons perched among trees
hunting along Normanskill
Albany/Bethlehem

Monarch Butterfly

If you would like to see a Monarch Butterfly, all you need to do is find a field of milkweeds, and in no time at all, you will be rewarded with the sight of one or more fluttering about from plant to plant.

The whole life cycle of the Monarch Butterfly is dependent upon milkweeds. So much so that Monarchs are sometimes called the "milkweed butterfly." Eggs laid on the plant grow into caterpillars that eat the leaves, flower buds, and milky juice. In both the caterpillar and butterfly stage, Monarch's need no camouflage because the milkweeds provide them with a unique defense. The plants contain a poisonous toxin that doesn't hurt the caterpillar, but makes the caterpillar poisonous for most predators to eat.

The Monarch is the only butterfly that migrates. In the late summer and fall, millions of Monarch Butterflies emerge from milkweed communities, flying as far as 3,000 miles to the mountains of Michoacan, Mexico, where they overwinter.

August 2006 Hot & sunny

Monarch
Butterfly

Milkweed
plants

Five Rivers Environmental Center

Sunflower

There are over fifty different species of Sunflowers native to North America, growing anywhere from 15 inches to 12 feet in height, in colors ranging from white, yellow, orange, bronze, and red. They are easy to grow, and can thrive in even the most neglected places, under adverse conditions. Sunflowers are an important source of sustenance for a variety of creatures.

Archeologists believe Native Americans used Sunflowers for food and medicine as long as 8,000 years ago. Seeds were roasted and ground into flour, or made into paste like peanut butter. Sunflower hulls were boiled in water to create a coffee-like drink, or made into a purple dye. Oil was extracted for cooking and hair treatment. The dried stalk was used as a building material. Sunflowers, believed to be sacred, were used in many ceremonies and rituals. Bowls filled with sunflower seeds were placed on graves to nourish the dead on their long journey into the afterlife.

Sunflowers symbolize warmth, loyalty, abundance, peace, and the will to persevere through difficult times.

August 2006
Hot & Sunny
Blue sky
Breezy

Sunflowers are
blooming, but not
in my backyard.
Every year that
I plant them, the
squirrels climb up
the stalk and chomp
until the flower heads
fall to the ground.

Gray Squirrel

Sunflower Seeds

Birdfeeders

Nature has a positive effect upon humans. It lifts our mood, engages our curiosity, and contributes to our overall psychological and physiological well-being. I spent this past weekend with someone who is not able to get out and about on a regular basis. Even so, we still found a way to enjoy nature together. Outside the front window was an array of feeders that attracted an interesting assortment of birds. It kept us amused for hours.

Sunflower seeds are popular with a wide range of birds. Suet attracts chickadees, woodpeckers, blue jays and sparrows. Finches and mourning doves love millet and thistle. You can feed some leftovers to birds. Small portions of cooked potatoes or rice, pieces of fruit and left over whole grain cereal are appropriate. But avoid giving anything made from white flour.

The optimal natural habitat provides food, shelter and a source of water. But even placing a few bird feeders adjacent to a window will bring feathered visitors into sight, benefiting both the viewer, and the birds.

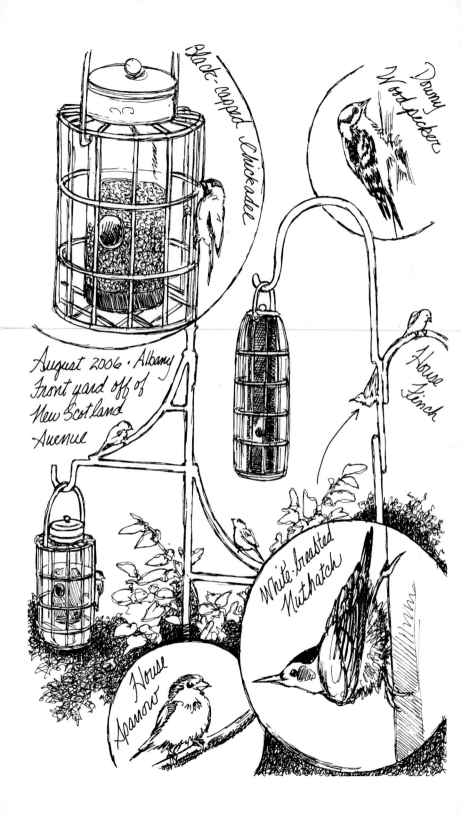

Black-capped Chickadee

Downy Woodpecker

House Finch

August 2006 · Albany
Front yard off of
New Scotland
Avenue

White-breasted
Nuthatch

House
Sparrow

Purple Loosestrife

Driving along the New York State Thruway, I noted an unfortunate beauty in full, late summer bloom. Purple Loosestrife, a tall, perennial plant, abundantly topped with showy spikes of purple flowers, is lovely to look at and a good source of nectar for bees. But it has few other redeeming qualities.

Purple Loosestrife is an invasive species, introduced to North America from Europe in the early 19th century. It is spreading rapidly because of its prolific seed production, increasing land development, and because it has no natural enemies here to keep it in check. This is causing great harm to local ecosystems as the species invades wetlands and fields, crowds out native plant communities, and threatens natural food sources for our local wildlife.

To date, there is no effective method to control Purple Loosestrife. Small amounts can be managed by mowing, burning or uprooting the plants by hand before they seed, or with herbicide application. Research is now underway to find natural enemies like insects to reduce it to tolerable levels.

Swampy wetlands along
Cemetery Road towards
Albany Rural Cemetary
Albany/Menands

August 2006

American
Goldfinch

Saw Honey Bees,
Monarch Butterfly
& Cardinal

Purple
Loosestrife

Great
Egret

submerged in duckweed & water

Lots of Darners
and Dragonflies
around

Red
Half-banded
Toper

Green Frog

Apples

As summer winds down and moves toward autumn, September kicks off the harvest season with apple picking. The old adage of "an apple a day keeps the doctor away" may be quite true. Studies have found that eating apples with skins prevents and fights cancer and heart disease. And New York is one of the top apple-producing states. So enjoy!

Apples are members of the rose family. Fossilized seed imprints prove their existence since the Neolithic period. But the fleshy, sweet, juicy fruit we eat today is much different than the earliest wild version, which was small, sour and full of seeds. Southwestern Asians and Romans first cultivated the fruit. The Romans introduced them to England. The Pilgrims introduced them to America. John Chapman from Massachusetts, also known as Johnny Appleseed, planted them throughout Illinois, Indiana, Kentucky, Pennsylvania and Ohio. In early America, most every farm grew apples. They are easy to grow and store, can be made into butter and cider, or dried for winter eating. And they taste great.

September 2006

Indian Ladders. Voorheesville
It's a wet and rainy
morning. Chilly.
One of my walking
companions,
a black lab,
decides to go
apple
picking.

Eyes on the prize!
→

Pileated Woodpecker

Old trees with large, oblong shaped holes, and wood chips scattered underneath, may indicate the presence of Pileated Woodpeckers excavating for food. Although they will eat fruits, nuts and sap, their main diet consists of Carpenter Ants. "Pileated" comes from the Latin word, "pileatus," meaning "wearing a cap," and refers to their distinctively shaped, red-headed crest.

A mated pair of Pileated Woodpeckers will remain together throughout the year. They spend their nights in separate roosting spots, but meet up around sunrise, staying within forty to fifty feet of each other, and calling out to keep in touch throughout the day. About an hour before sunset, they return to their separate roosting spots.

The largest of the species in North America, Pileated Woodpeckers need a great range of territory, and mature, sparsely populated forests. Because of the total clearing of old growth forests for farming and lumbering at the turn of the century, they were rarely seen in the Northeast. But as forests have regrown and aged, the Pileated Woodpecker has returned.

Mother & babies spotted last Spring in Albany New Scotland Avenue

September 2006

Sunny but cool.

A group of juvenile Pileated Woodpeckers climb about and drum on a phone pole.

Near the Normanskill River

Thump! Thump! Thump! Thump!

Fungi/Mushrooms

There is a diverse beauty in the shapes and colors of mushrooms. These fungi are interesting to look at, and have an important role in the continuous rebirth of nature.

Fungi are made up of microscopic webs of thread-like filaments called "hyphae" and "mycelium." These networks remain hidden under decaying organic matter, such as rotted wood, bark, leaves or animals, drawing in and then returning nutrients to the soil. The mushroom is the fruit, or the visible part of the fungus, which reproduces by releasing spores.

Fungi share some characteristics of plants, but lack chlorophyll, so they do not photosynthesize. Fungi also share some characteristics of animals. Their cell walls are built out of the same material as the hard outer shells of insects and other arthropods. Being neither plant nor animal, Fungi are a classification of living organisms unto themselves. Mushrooms, puff-balls, rust, lichens, mold and yeast are all members of the Fungi Kingdom. There are over 72,000 species, and millions more as yet waiting to be discovered.

Fungi · Mushrooms

Coral type of fungi along Normanskill

A circle of mushrooms on a stretch of grass in downtown Albany — called a fairy ring.

Mushrooms in the Adirondacks

Puff balls along Indian ladder trail
Press them and brown powder puffs out

Poison Ivy

While walking in the woods, I came across a stand of trees with large, woody, ropelike vines climbing them. The vines were covered with coarse, hairy, reddish colored roots. I had never seen anything like them before. Thank goodness I didn't touch them. They were Poison Ivy.

Poison Ivy's oily sap produces a chemical, called Urushiol, which causes a rash, blisters and uncomfortable itch. Although Poison Ivy can grow as a bush, shrub or creeping vine, it usually has three leaflets with pointed tips. The saying "leaves of three, let it be" is a reminder to avoid contact with the plant.

I wondered if people would recognize these woody vines without their fall foliage as Poison Ivy? People have unknowingly collected this less recognized form to make into holiday wreaths, suffering the consequences. Burning it as firewood has caused rashes or serious lung irritations via smoke. Maybe we should come up with a second warning: "Vines so hairy, very scary?" Well, maybe I need to work on that one a bit…

Helderberg Mountains

Poison Ivy

September 2006. Cold & rainy. The season is definitely changing. I came upon these curious looking vines...

Canada Geese

In the dark of the night, I heard the call of Canada Geese in flight. Long after they had passed overhead, I continued to visualize their V-shaped formation journeying south for the winter, comforted by nature's predictable cycle.

The cues for migration are not known for sure. It could be changing weather conditions, dwindling food supplies, or hormones, which are affected by shortened daylight hours. Most flocks begin practicing flights and landings in September, finally leaving for their long migration by mid October. They follow the same migration route every year, traveling thousands of miles by day and night, using landmarks and the stars to navigate their way.

In flight, the V-formation is like a race, usually led by the loudest and most aggressive male or female bird, with smaller, more subservient birds following towards the back. Once the leader is exhausted, the next strongest bird takes over the front position.

Canada Geese mate and care for each other throughout their whole life. If one of the pair is injured or dies, the other will linger nearby.

Last week of
September — I hear
honking and look up to see the
familiar V-formation of geese
in migration.

A flock of
Canadian Geese
land in a cut down
cornfield along
Route 2 near
Eagle Mills
NY

Woolly Bear Caterpillar

On a recent warm October day, a slew of fuzzy, black and copper colored caterpillars called Woolly Bears seemingly sprinted across my path, scurrying in haste to find shelter for themselves before the onset of winter. I gathered one up to watch it curl into a ball in my hand, splaying its hairy bristles that most predators find unappetizing to the outside, and protecting its vulnerable underside within. The following spring, this caterpillar will emerge from hibernation, spin a cocoon, and metamorphose into the Isabella Tiger Moth.

According to folklore, Woolly Bear caterpillars with wide copper bands of color forecast a mild winter, and those with narrow copper bands forecast a long, harsh winter. But in actuality, the amount of color is attributed to age, with young Woolly Bears having more black and a narrower copper band in their middle, and these bands widening as the caterpillar matures. When early winters set in, less mature caterpillars look for shelter sooner than usual. This may be where the superstition originated.

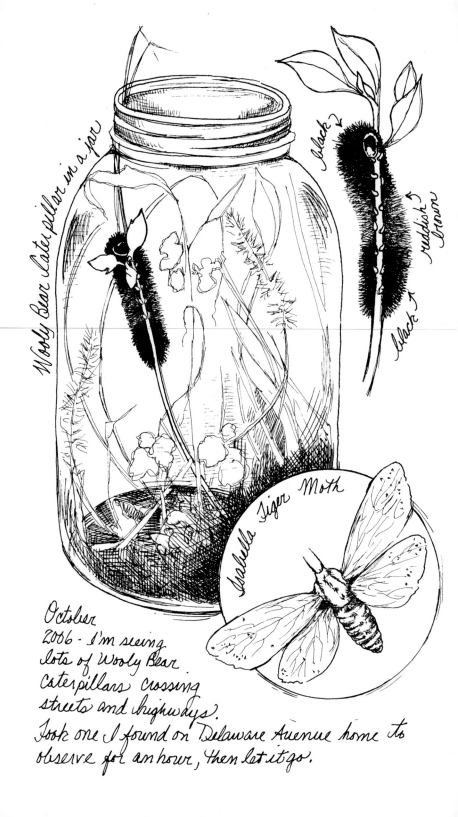

Wooly Bear Caterpillar in a jar

black?

black

reddish brown

Isabella Tiger Moth

October
2006 - I'm seeing
lots of Wooly Bear
Caterpillars crossing
streets and highways.
Took one I found on Delaware Avenue home to
observe for an hour, then let it go.

Pumpkins

Widely recognized as the icons of fall, Pumpkins are characterized by tough stalks, vines with spring-like tendrils, grayish-green leaves and fleshy, orange fruit. They are members of the gourd family (cucurbitaceae), which includes other types of squash, luffa, cucumbers and melons.

Archaeological evidence indicates that pumpkins have been cultivated in the Americas by indigenous people for thousands of years. Colonial settlers sliced the tops off, removed the seeds, filled them with milk, spices and honey and roasted them in the hot ashes of their fires, a precursor to pumpkin pie.

Carving jack-o-lanterns originated from an ancient pagan festival that marked the last harvest before the beginning of the cold, dark winter. Fearing the realm of spirits, people carved lanterns from turnips, beets or potatoes, placed burning coals inside, and set them in their windows and doorways for protection. Remnants from this festival continue today with All Soul's Day and Halloween. Irish immigrants arriving in America found pumpkins easy to carve, and thus was born the tradition we carry on today.

October 2006

Oak Leaves

Autumn leaves have passed their color peak, but I still enjoy picking them up off the ground to inspect their variant shades, shapes and nuances. I have been noticing different oak leaves all week. This may be because oak leaves contain tannin, once used for tanning and dying leather, and decompose more slowly than other tree leaves.

Oak trees are members of the Beech family. Their seeds develop from female flowers that bloom in spring, then take one full year to ripen into acorns that fall to the ground in the fall. Oaks are slow growing, living 200 to 400 years, and do not bear acorns until about 20 years. They have the strongest and most durable wood.

I have a red oak and a white oak in my yard which I never planted myself. Squirrels, blue jays and woodpeckers hide acorns underground, or under leaves. Some are retrieved later in the winter season when food is scarce. Some become rotten and moldy. And some sprout to regenerate new oak trees.

White Oak Acorn

Five Rivers
Delmar

September 2006

Red
Oak

White Oak
Albany
Delaware
Ave. Area

Common Loon

It's always a thrill for me to hear the haunting, melancholy yodel, or maniacal laugh, of the Common Loon during a summer overnight in the Adirondack Mountains. These elusive birds prefer quiet, secluded northern lakes during breeding season. On rare sightings, I'd watch them dive and swim for long distances underwater before popping up in another area.

Loons begin migrating to coastal areas from September through November, with large numbers of them stopping to rest and feed at the Great Lakes. Their black and white summer plumage will dramatically molt to duller gray and white feathers for the winter months.

I was disheartened to learn recently of large bird kills on Lake Ontario. Hundreds, perhaps thousands, of birds died from Botulism, most likely contracted through invasive zebra mussels eaten by fish, which were then eaten by the birds. Many were Loons, already threatened by the effects of mercury poisoning, acid rain and increased human development and activity in their breeding grounds. Loons are on the NYS Department of Conservation's "Special Concern" list.

Wildlife Pathology Lab   October 2006
9:30 am
Cold
Delmar NY

Wing
juvenile Loon

Adult Loon
with summer
plumage

Starlings

Starlings are robin sized, short tailed, black feathered birds, with hints of green and purple iridescence to their plumage. The name Starling means "little star," and refers to the white speckles they develop during the fall and winter months. These disappear again by spring.

Their beaks are strongest when opening, rather than shutting. Digging into soil, their jaws spring open to expose the insects and larvae they like to eat.

Starlings live and travel in large communal groups throughout the year, and can reach overwhelming numbers. They are not native to our country. In 1890, an eccentric drug manufacturer named Eugene Scheiffelin, released sixty European Starlings into New York City's Central Park, and another forty the following year. Enamored with the works of William Shakespeare, he wanted to introduce all the birds the playwright mentioned in his works into the United States. All Starlings that now populate North America are descendants of that first small group that built their nests under the eves of the Museum of Natural History.

November · European Starlings

On wires
in trees
and on lawns

Noisy & conspicuous.

"Nay, I'll have a starling shall be
taught to speak nothing but
Mortimer, and give it its him
to keep his anger still in motion" – Shakespear "Henry IV"

3 Bugs

This morning at work, an eastern box elder crawled across my computer keyboard. These bugs feed on pod bearing box elder trees and maples. Other than producing stains and an unpleasant odor when crushed, they do no harm. But they can become invasive in the fall, crawling into buildings through cracks and open crevices.

In the afternoon, I noticed an odd looking bug jumping conspicuously on the pavement and identified it as a backswimmer, an aquatic insect that swims upside down. How it arrived in our landlocked parking lot is a mystery. I am very lucky I handled it carefully, as I later learned their bite is as painful as a bee sting.

That night, a house centipede scampered quickly across my living room floor. They prefer damp environments like basements and unexcavated areas under the house. Although scary looking, house centipedes are harmless and beneficial to your home, feeding voraciously on more damaging insects, larvae and spiders.

Three interesting insect encounters in one day is plenty enough for me!

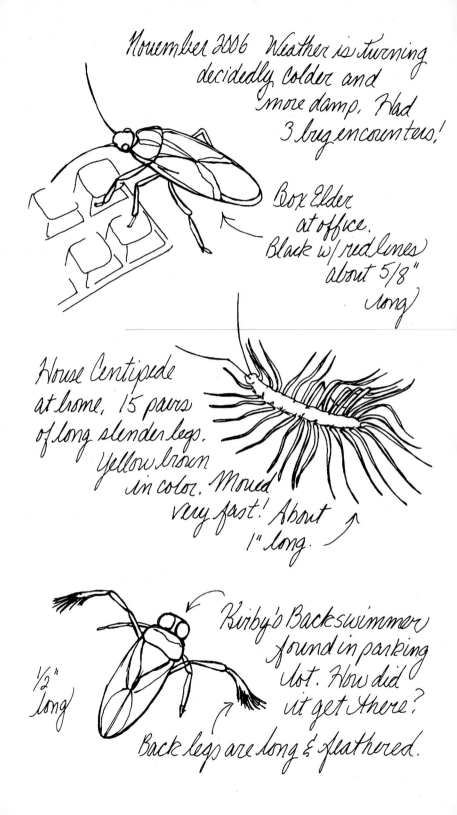

November 2006 Weather is turning decidedly colder and more damp. Had 3 bug encounters!

Box Elder at office. Black w/ red lines about 5/8" long

House Centipede at home. 15 pairs of long slender legs. Yellow brown in color. Moved very fast! About 1" long.

Kirby's Backswimmer found in parking lot. How did it get there?

1/2" long

Back legs are long & feathered.

Wild Turkey

The main attraction of Thanksgiving dinner is not the same bird as the wild turkey you see in the woods and more rural areas. Wild turkeys are thinner than domesticated turkeys, and can fly for short distances at speeds up to 55 miles per hour. Domesticated turkeys cannot fly at all.

Native to North America, wild turkeys were a major source of food for Native Americans, and for the first settlers. But due to over-hunting and deforestation, they disappeared completely from New York State by the mid-1840's. It took another hundred years before wild turkeys were re-established in the state through the efforts of conservationists.

In the fall and winter, wild turkeys form large flocks, searching for beechnuts, acorns, berries and grains to eat by day, and roosting in trees at night. During snowstorms, you'll see them perched on branches, waiting out the weather. Turkeys can scratch through half a foot of snow to find food. In addition to its famous "gobble," wild turkeys have 28 different calls.

Saw wild turkeys in Altamont & along the Normanskill River.

Wild Turkey feather

Even saw a pair roosting in a pine tree in my Albany backyard!

November 2006

Burdock

A brief excursion outdoors amongst autumn's dried plants might cause you to find yourself covered in sticky seeds and burs that cling firmly to your clothing. Whether you find this amusing, or mildly annoying, stop a moment and think about this ingenious way that nature works to increase its chances of survival.

Common burdock is a biennial weed that grows wild throughout North America, Europe and Asia. It produces large, heart-shaped, hairy leaves and red-violet flowers that resemble thistle, but are differentiated by barbed bracts that form on marble sized burs. These easily detach and adhere to whatever passes by.

Upon returning from a hike, a Swiss engineer named George de Mestral was intrigued by the burs that stuck to his wool trousers and dog's fur. Looking at the burs through a microscope, he noted tiny hooks at the end of each spike, and was inspired to create a fastening system based upon the design. Combining the words "velour" and "crochet" (French for "velvet" and "hooks"), he patented Velcro in 1955.

November 2006   1pm Sunny & warm.

Birds
very
active
today!

Common Burdock →

Seeds &
burs stick
to my
clothes ← Beggar's Tick

Lone Blue Jay – very busy flitting
from tree to tree, searching in grass

Winter Bird Flocks

Along a thicketed forest edge, bordering a field, I stopped to watch a flock of small, sociable, energetic birds foraging and calling out to each other. The group was mainly made up of black-capped chickadees and tufted titmice, but with them I noticed a pair of tiny birds I had never seen before. They looked like plump, feathered spheres amongst the twigs and branches.

At first I thought they were hurt, because they were fidgeting and flicking their wings. But this observation actually helped me to identify them later as golden-crowned kinglets. I learned that they are sometimes called "butterfly birds" because of their "quick and fluttery" flight as they forage. They fluff up their plumage to stay warm, which gives them the rounded appearance.

In the winter, it is common for these mixed species bird groups to form. In addition to black-capped chickadees, tufted titmice and kinglets, downy woodpeckers and nuthatches may also join. This winter flocking behavior may increase foraging efficiency and better detection of potential predators.

December 2006 Cold & brisk.
Flock of small birds flitting
and foraging along the woodline.

Black capped chickadee

Tufted Titmouse

Deer tracks in the
mud. I look up to
see a lone
doe.

Kinglet?

Tiny, plump,
round birds.
I've never seen
them before. Flutters
and flicks feathers.

Pine Barrens

Pine barrens are wide, rolling landscapes, densely covered with pitch pines, prairie grass, and shrubs that are deeply rooted in soft, sandy dunes of nutrient poor soil. With their minimal water supply, dry conditions make them prone to periodic fires. But the plants and animals that live there are ecologically adapted to this, and in some cases, fires are necessary for certain species to survive. Pine barren ecosystems are critically imperiled on a global scale. Yet we have one right in our own backyard.

When the last glaciers in New York State melted over 15,000 years ago, a massive lake formed where Abany, Colonie and Guilderland now border each other, depositing sand which is the foundation of the Albany Pine Bush preserve. This habitat supports a unique variety of plants and animals. Some species, such as the blue spotted salamander, eastern hognose snake, spotted turtle and the karner blue butterfly, are rare or seriously endangered. It is my hope that this precious treasure be preserved, conserved and diligently guarded from over-development.

December 2006 · Dusk at Pine Bush Preserve

Cold — but still no snow!

The scraggly pines in silhouette remind me of Japanese woodblock prints. Other than the whir of highway traffic and hunter's gunfire in the distance, all is very still and quiet. Coyote prints in the soft dune sand let me know I'm not alone.

Muskrat

Muskrats are semi-aquatic mammals that are well adapted to living in and around rivers, streams, ditches, marshes or ponds. They are excellent swimmers because of their partially webbed hind feet with stiff fringes of hair between the toes, which work like paddles, and their long, flattened tail that is used like a rudder for steering. They can remain submerged under water for up to 15 minutes.

Muskrats are closely related to beavers, but are not as large. They are about the size of a cottontail rabbit or your family cat. Muskrats build dome shaped lodges that are similar to a beaver's, but smaller in scale. They also burrow dens into shoreline banks. But muskrats do not build dams.

Active throughout the winter, muskrats live mostly in darkness within their lodges or dens, feeding nocturnally on the roots and stems of aquatic plants like cattail, sedge, bulrush and arrowhead. You might spy one venturing outside to feed by water's edge at dawn or dusk. Occasionally, they also eat crayfish, mussels and fish.

December 2006 Buckingham Pond · Albany
The sun has just set. All is
enveloped in shadow.

It has been
unseasonably warm.
But tonight, a thin sheet of
ice forms on the water.
In the distance, a muskrat
feeds while sitting on a
log. It hears me, and
with a splash, plunges into the icy
depths and swims swiftly away.

White Footed Mouse

The most common mice in the northeast are the deer mouse and white-footed mouse, which are native to our country, and the house mouse, which was introduced. Native mice live in wooded, brushy or marshy areas. But during the winter season, more opportunistic mice may seek shelter in or about human dwellings.

Mice are active year-round. For the most part, they are nocturnal. Some are solitary except during the breeding season, and some live together sharing a nest, especially for warmth during colder weather. Their food cache may consist of nuts, seeds, greens, berries, insects and household food scraps. They are very agile, and can leap and climb, using their tails for balance. Nests may be built under woodpiles or brush, in abandoned bird or squirrel nests, tree hollows, and within the walls of your house.

Mice play a critical role in the food chain, providing sustenance for hawks, owls, snakes, foxes, skunks, coyotes, weasels and maybe even your family cat. A healthy mouse population ensures that other wildlife will survive.

End of December 2006
Still no snow...
No chance to get
out to view
nature this
week. But
some nature
got inside to
view me.

White-footed Mouse

The cats
were nosing
around the base of our holiday
tree. Upon closer inspection, I
saw what I thought was a stuffed
animal, or ornament. Then it blinked!

Fossils

Rare fossils are found in museums, but many common fossils can also be found in abundance locally. I've unearthed them by streambeds, found them inside rocks, along the cliffs of the Helderberg Mountains, and with gravel put down for driveways from local quarries. Look closely at the rock border by the Post Office in Stuyvesant Plaza and you'll find them there too.

These fossils are the remains of organisms from millions of years ago that are now extinct. Buried deep in the mud of the shallow seas that once covered New York State during the Paleozoic Era, they eventually compressed and hardened, leaving preserved impressions of shells, and clues to other internal structures of life forms from an ancient time. New York's official state fossil is the eurypterid, or sea scorpion.

Primitive peoples, who could not explain the strange fossil images, attributed supernatural powers to them, even wearing them as amulets. Others have thought they were unsuccessful forms of life discarded by a "creator," or remnants from the great biblical flood.

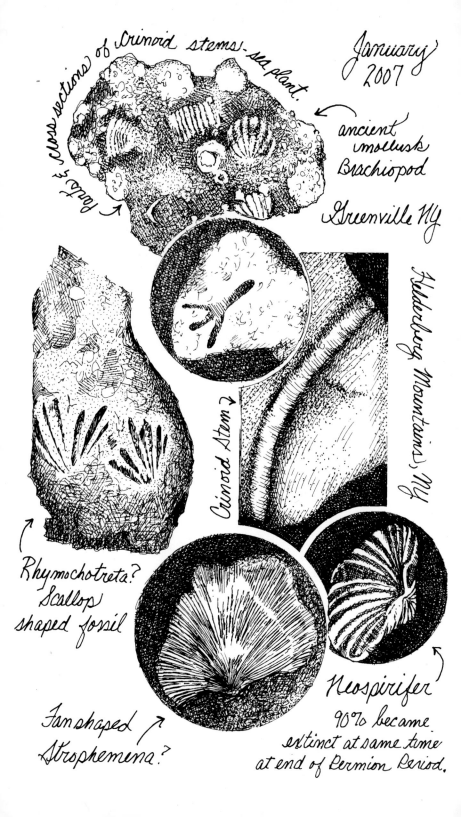

parts & cross sections of Crinoid stems - sea plant.

January 2007

← ancient mollusk Brachiopod

Greenville NY

← Helderberg Mountains, NY

Crinoid Stem ?

Rhynchotreta? Scallop shaped fossil

Fan shaped ↗ Strophemena ?

Neospirifer
90% became extinct at same time at end of Permion Period.

Pigeons/Rock Doves

Reviled as pests, called dumb, and even referred to as "flying rats," the much-maligned pigeon deserves a revisionist description. City pigeons actually descend from rock doves that inhabit rocky seaside cliffs and desert canyons throughout Eurasia. Since their introduction to our country about 400 years ago, they have adapted remarkably to urban living, using buildings, ledges, rooftops, steeples and attics as replacements for their natural habitats.

Most pigeons have red feet and orange eyes. But there are many variations in feather coloration, from gray and white with iridescence, to blue-gray, reddish, speckled or solid-colored. Because of their strong homing instincts, pigeons have been bred, domesticated and used as messengers throughout history. Scientists know very little about city pigeons. Perhaps they are taken for granted.

Try a more appreciative thought about the resourceful pigeons that sun themselves on buildings in the city. Many people enjoy quiet moments feeding them in the park. While waiting at the bus stop, watching a pigeon's forward-backward head-bobbing strut may even amuse you enough to make you smile.

Pigeons / Rock Doves

January 2007
Unusually warm.

Pigeons sun themselves on rooftops along Delaware Avenue in Albany.

But disappear when it rains.

Crows

Crows are members of the Corvid family, which also includes ravens, blue jays, and magpies. Social, vocal and territorial, they are considered one of the most intelligent of all bird species.

Crows mate for life, forming tight-knit family flocks. Juveniles don't mate until after spending a few seasons living cooperatively with their parents and other crows, helping to raise successive fledglings, defend against predators, and learning survival skills. As omnivores, crows consume insects, larvae, worms, fruits, grains, and nuts, and also scavenge food from garbage and road kill. Crows can live up to twenty years.

During winter, crows gather at night in roosts that range in size from the hundreds up to the thousands. I have always enjoyed watching for them at dusk, gathering from all directions and long distances along the same flight lines towards the neighborhood wood lot where they formed a roost of 30,000. Recently, hand-held lasers, pyrotechnics and recorded distress calls were used to scare them away because of complaints by those who found them inconvenient and annoying.

January 2007 - Finally some icy, winter-like weather arrived.

"I speak for the Crows!"

Tree branches once filled with the dark silhouettes of thousands of crows, are now silent, stark and bare. Professionals have scattered and scared them away. Crows have gathered in Albany's University Heights for hundreds of years. Maybe since the 1800's, when it was an almshouse cemetery.

Recent development, bulldozing a pond, destruction of woods & fields, has disrupted and displaced nature. An oasis within city limits is disappearing fast. More foresight would entail a change in the attitude of people, rather than crow behavior.

I am reminded of the passenger pigeon. Once common & abundant, they are now extinct. For the greater wants of human beings, not a single passenger pigeon remains on Earth.

Evergreens

The blazing color of autumn's deciduous trees long gone, those branches now crisscross in stark, bare, leafless patterns against a dull, gray sky. Because of low air humidity, little sun absorption, and frozen soil making it impossible to draw water through roots and conserve it, deciduous trees lose their leaves in the fall and become dormant to survive winter.

It is the blue-greens of evergreens that catch our eyes now. The waxy coatings on their leaves and needles seal moisture inside, protect against freezing and keep water loss at a minimum. Although they lose their leaves and needles too, it occurs unobtrusively throughout the entire year, and is hardly noticeable. Steeple shapes better absorb sunlight, and bendable branches shed heavy snow without breaking.

Evergreens were the first trees to appear on our planet, providing food and shelter for many species. Placed strategically around buildings, evergreens intercept cold winds, help conserve energy and reduce heating costs. Evergreens have long been thought to have magical powers - perhaps to conjure the coming of spring.

I watch for evergreens
against the
winter white & grey.

Cedar

Holly

White Pine

Pachysandra

Hemlock.

January 2007 Very cold. Finally, a light
dusting of snow is on the ground.

Sugar Maple

Pure maple syrup is unique to North America. Especially in the northeast, where maples prefer the gradual seasonal change to colder weather in the fall, reaching a dormant cessation of growth in winter called "hardening." Sugar produced in leaves through summertime photosynthesis is stored inside tree trunks until the winter freeze ends. As spring nears, temperatures slowly and gradually ease back and forth between warmer days and freezing nights. The sugar dissolves into the sap, while pressure builds, triggering the sap to flow. This is called "sugaring off" weather, the best time to tap the maple trees for syrup.

After Vermont and Maine, New York is the third major supplier of maple syrup. For generations, maple sugar was tapped between mid-February to early March, ending in early April. In recent years though, with first frosts arriving later in autumn, gradual increases in average annual temperature, and more erratic weather fluctuations, maple syrup producers have been forced to tap their trees earlier and earlier in the season, sometimes even in January.

Trees in Winter   January 2007

Five Rivers,
Delmar

Sugar Maple Trees

Most Maple trees have opposite branches. Maple branches are thin. Bark develops rough vertical grooves as it ages.

State tree of N.Y.
Hardest and strongest wood of the maple tree family.

Maple Syrup!

Winged Seeds

Owls

Creatures of the night, owls symbolize wisdom, stealth, and the ability to navigate darkness. In our region, listen for the haunting calls of barred owls, screech owls, and great horned owls in the early evenings and pre-dawn hours of February, when they are defending their territory and advertising for mates.

Owls have interesting adaptations that help them hunt at night. Large eyes, with light receiving rod cells, make for optimal night vision. Binocular vision allows them to see three dimensionally. Keen hearing, with one ear slightly higher than the other, allows sound to be heard from above and below. Owl feathers direct sound to their face, and are structured for silent flight, making it easy for them to sweep down upon unsuspecting prey.

Owls have no predators other than other larger owls, and humans. They are sometimes killed by power lines, or struck by cars as they swoop down at night. Between owls and daytime raptors, mice and other small rodent populations are kept in check, ensuring natures delicate balance.

February
2007
Owl Walk
at Pine
Barren
Preserve

Screech
Owl

Barred Owl

Didn't see
any owls. But
I heard some
faint
calls.

Great Horned Owl

House Sparrow

Birds in the beginning throes of courtship become more apparent in February. One of the more conspicuous is the male house sparrow. To attract a potential mate, he sings an insistent, rhythmic and repetitive chirping song, advertising a suitable nest site he's found. When a female approaches, his song quickens and becomes louder. He follows her, hops about, quivers his wings and flies in and out of his nest site to gain her attention.

House sparrows are monogamous for the breeding season, and usually raise two or more broods. They prefer to nest in the crevices and cavities of buildings, or build domed nests with a small side entrance in trees, shrubs or dense vines. The nest often contains grass, feathers, bits of trash, string and paper.

The house sparrow was one of the 100 species of birds that were introduced into America from Europe, released in New York City between 1850 and 1851. They originated from Eurasia and northern Africa. House sparrows can aggressively out-compete native birds for nesting sites.

February
2007
Albany, NY

Male
House Sparrows
stake out
nests in the
nooks and
crannies of
old buildings
along Broadway
Downtown

Snow

Frozen water represents 80% of all freshwater on Earth. Melted snow runoff feeds streams, rivers and groundwater, and powers our own great Hudson River. A substantial amount of melted snow is needed to stave off drought conditions in the upcoming warmer seasons. Rainfall alone isn't enough.

Snow insulates dormant vegetation from below zero degree weather, and stores moisture for seeds and root systems until they are ready for germination and re-growth in the spring. What doesn't evaporate provides the garden's first spring watering. Small mammals like mice, voles and muskrats create networks of tunnels underneath the snow, allowing them to move from one food source to another without exposure to predators. It also allows above snow level mammals to reach higher to the bark and twigs they couldn't eat before.

We've just dug out from our first, and maybe only, significant snowfall of the season. Whether you regard it as a recreational pleasure, an aesthetic beauty, or an inconvenient disruption, snow is important.

February 2007 A whole season's worth of snow was dumped in one day! Cold too!

But there are buds on the pear tree, and Tufted Titmice in my backyard preparing for Spring.

House plants

Houseplants bring tangible life-giving energy into our home and workplace. A growing amount of scientific and academic research proves that houseplants are beneficial to our health.

The indoor environments of man-made buildings, furnishings and other materials, which include adhesives, paints, carpets, synthetics, computer screens, photocopiers and printing machinery, expose us to harmful chemicals, emissions and pollutants. Houseplants help absorb and remove these toxins. They purify and renew stale air, turn exhaled carbon dioxide into fresh oxygen through transpiration, and raise humidity. Houseplants also promote healing and recovery, reduce headaches and fatigue, lower blood pressure and promote feelings of relaxation and calm.

If you are homebound this winter or throughout the year, or just confined to an office for long periods of time, keep a few houseplants nearby. Some of the most beneficial houseplants to keep indoors are ficus, ivy, spider plant, philodendrons, peace lilies, potted chrysanthemums, ferns, dragon tree and palms. Take time to notice their beauty, knowing they are also promoting good health, improving air quality and increasing your well being.

February/March 2007

Spider Plants

Aloe Plant

Christmas cactus bloom!

More snow. Cold and
icy outside. Inside
greenery cheers me.

Birdwatching Cats

A curious behavior to observe in a pet cat is when it is making that distinctive chattering noise at birds or a squirrel just out of reach through a window, or on television. As cats are normally completely silent when stalking and hunting, it could just be an expression of frustration and excitement at seeing prey they cannot access. Some say the sound causes curiosity in the creature being stalked, so that it will overcome its caution and approach within easy ambush range. Most likely though, the "chattering" is actually a simulation of an instinctual neck bite cats use to efficiently make a quick kill of a bird or small rodent before it has a chance to struggle and get away.

Cats will hiss, growl, caterwaul, shriek, and use scent, facial expressions, complex body language and touch to communicate with each other. It is interesting to note though, that other than between a mother cat and its kittens, adult cats use meowing exclusively to communicate with humans, and not with each other.

March 2007

Pre-spring activity going on outside.

Despite the cold and ice...

My cats are bird watching at the window

Woodchuck

Woodchucks are short-legged, round eared, bushy tailed, slow moving, burrowing rodents that can grow up two feet long and appear quite fat. The word woodchuck originates from the Native American word "wuchak," and describes a variety of animals of similar size and color. They are also called groundhogs or marmots.

Woodchucks inhabit farm fields, open meadows, and woodland edges. Their long claws are well adapted for digging the network of underground tunnels, runways and rooms that make up their burrows. Different areas have different purposes. For instance, one may be used for sleeping, another for hibernation, another for birthing, and another just for toilet use. Woodchucks feed on tender vegetation, such as grasses, clover and alfalfa. They love to bask in the sun.

The February legend of Groundhog Day actually originated in Europe, involving either a hedgehog or badger, and has no basis in fact. Most woodchucks are active in the spring and summer, disappear sometime after August to hibernate for the winter, and do not come out of hibernation until March.

March 2007 · 5:30 pm. Clocks set ahead. It's lighter
out after work. First walk down by the Normanskill
River since the snows. Wet. Slushy. The sounds of
water. Reddish brown fur and some movement
under tangled brambles catches my eye.
A wood chuck – awakened
from hibernation.
Spring is near!

Two robins flit about
a tree down by the river

Gulls on the Hudson

Gulls inhabit many aquatic environments, not just the ocean. Large flocks can be seen in local mall and restaurant parking lots, and around the Albany garbage dump. On a recent walk along the Hudson River, I spotted a large flock riding the ice floes.

Generally, with their gregarious nature and easily recognizable piercing cry, gulls are conspicuously easy to identify. Yet, with similarities between species, and wide variations of appearance even within a species, identifying the specific name can be challenging. Further complicating the matter, gulls have variations in seasonal plumage, and young gulls go through yearly appearance changes for three to four years before they reach adult plumage.

The gulls I saw had white heads, gray backs and black tipped wings with white spots. Some of the gulls seemed small with a relatively short bill. They were too far away for me to gauge any distinguishing marks in detail, but the end of the bills seemed dark. I narrowed it down to either ring-billed or herring gulls, or a mixed crew.

March 2007

Albany - Along the Hudson River

Gulls

Vernal Ponds

Vernal ponds form in March and April when snow melts and spring rains gather and fill the shallow, natural depressions of level ground. These ephemeral wetlands are seasonally finite bodies of water that generally dry up by summer or early autumn. A quiet drama is now taking place as wetland dwellers race to meet nature's vital timetable of reproduction.

Because they are by definition devoid of fish, vernal ponds provide critical breeding habitat for wood frogs; marbled, spotted and blue spotted salamanders; and fairy shrimp. This specialized ecosystem allows them to safely breed and reproduce, and reduces the danger of their vulnerable offspring being eaten by predators. Vernal pools are also vital for spring peepers, tree frogs, dragonflies, damselflies, snakes, turtles, and many species of birds and plants. Some species breed nowhere else.

Because vernal ponds are small, often isolated, and dry for most of the year, many people don't recognize their importance. Some vernal ponds are incredibly old. All are part of an annual cycle that the natural world depends upon.

March
April
2007

In the
moist woods
of the
Helderberg
Mtns.

Black with yellow spots.

Spotted
Salamanders

Live mostly underground
throughout the year. Emerge
in March and April during
snow melt and rainfall, when
temperatures reach 50° or more.
Spotted Salamanders can
live up to 20 years.

Skunk

Skunks are reclusive members of the weasel family. They are nocturnal omnivores, foraging from night to dawn for berries, grasses, nuts, worms, insects, grubs, amphibians and small rodents. You can sometimes find evidence of their nightly activity when they leave holes in the ground from digging or tearing apart the ground nests of small animals.

The Latin name for striped skunk is Mephitis mephitis, which aptly means "double foul odor." Sighting the distinctively bold black and white coloration is enough to warn anyone familiar enough with the reason for its namesake to either proceed or retreat with caution.

When a skunk becomes agitated or fearful, it will stamp its feet, growl and hiss, and finally raise its tail to spray an extremely potent, powerfully scented and disagreeable acidic musk from glands below. This secretion can cause mild irritation to severe headache, nausea, vomiting, and painful burning of nostrils and eyes, and may even cause temporary blindness. A skunk can spray up to 15 feet away, and the odor can carry for miles.

April 2007 The weather warms. Mornings are filled with the calls of Cardinals, Tufted Titmice, Mourning Doves and Sparrows. Today I caught a whiff of the distinctive scent of skunk. Later, saw dead skunk along 9W in Glenmont.

Striped
Skunk

Dark-eyed Junco

The dark-eyed junco (Junco hyemalis) is a two-toned gray bird with dark eyes, a pinkish, conical shaped bill and outer tail feathers that flash a white V-shape upon flight. There are five distinctively different varieties that can be identified regionally, but all are considered to be the same sparrow-related species. Our northeastern version is the slate-colored junco, distinguished by a darker charcoal colored hood on its head.

Juncos breed, nest and raise their young in Canada and the northern United States, but head south to warmer weather in the winter, arriving in most northern states when it starts to snow, and migrating back north when the snows melt each spring. This earned them the nickname "snowbird."

This week I noticed small flocks of junco's foraging on the ground amongst the leaves and weeds in my yard, probably en route in migration. They have a curious way of double-scratching the earth with both feet simultaneously to expose seeds and insects to eat, even when food is right there in front of them.

Pussy Willows · Slingerlands

Crocuses
Pine Hills · Albany

"Beneath, it's snowy mantle cold and clean,
The unborn grass lies waiting for it's coat to turn its green.
The snowbird sings the song he always sings,
And speaks to me of flowers that will bloom again in spring."
- Anne Murray 1970

April 2007

Slate-colored Dark-eyed Junco's in my Albany yard.

Mourning Dove

A symbol of spirit, wisdom, counsel and piety, the slender mourning dove is an elegant sight both in the wild and at the birdfeeder. Between dawn and dusk, listen for their sad, plaintive "wh'hooo, hoo, hoo, hooo," the soulful call for which they are named.

A long version of the call is given throughout the breeding season by unmated males trying to establish territory and attract a mate. A shorter version of the call indicates a mated pair may be building their nest nearby. These are the main two calls of the mourning dove. Although, their wings make a soft whistle-whirring sound as they take flight.

Mourning doves prefer building their nest on a platform of loose twigs and grass in elm, maple or coniferous trees, about 10 to 30 feet above ground. They may raise between two to five clutches per year. Both parents are involved in all aspects of breeding, with the male usually on the nest from morning until evening, and the female taking over from evening until dawn.

April
2007

Cold weather, sleet, snow &
rain has swept through
the area. Yet the birds
remain quite active
and vocal.

No matter what,
a new mating &
nesting season is
under way!

Mourning Doves

In my
Albany yard &
the Castleton area.

Forsythia

The often overlooked, yet miraculous, event of buds bursting open on trees and shrubs is happening all around you this week. But if you're not paying attention, you might miss it.

All dormant buds contain the necessary ingredients to bloom every spring, but it's a complex process that is still not fully understood by scientists. The length of days, moisture levels and temperature are all factors that initiate the process. And every plant is different. A tree in one neighborhood may already have sprouted, while another one down the street may not have done so yet.

One of the earliest buds to burst in spring is the forsythia. All over our area, I've noticed their graceful, cascading branches covered from ground to tip with a profusion of yellow blossoms, bursting into bloom. Related to Oleaceae, the olive family, forsythia are mostly native to Asia, but were introduced in America about 100 years ago. People started calling them forsythia on honor of William Forsyth, a Scottish botanist who lived between 1737 and 1804.

April 2007

Buds are
beginning
to burst
open.
Brilliant
yellow
flowers
everywhere.

Forsythia

Robins and Earthworms

In watching a tug of war between a robin and an earthworm, the earthworm seems surprisingly strong. Yet the effort is worth the struggle for the robin. Earthworms are a rich source of protein for insect-eating birds and mammals. Why is it so difficult for the robin to pull up the worm?

An earthworm's body is divided into 100 or more segments that alternately thicken and contract in successive muscular waves. On the side of each segment are tiny, claw-like bristles called setae. When earthworms shorten themselves, the setae push outward against their earthen burrow walls to propel themselves in either direction. When earthworms extend themselves, the setae pull in, and a secretion of slimy lubricating mucus helps them slide through the soil.

As a robin begins to pull an earthworm out of the ground, the setae bristles stay anchored inside the burrow. Sometimes the struggle is so matched that the worm breaks apart. Depending on where the break occurs, the earthworm may regenerate itself, growing back a new head or segments.

Stopped to make some quick sketches of the robin whs has been singing, bathing and dining in my Albany yard.

April / May 2007

Woodland Flowers

Woodland flowers were beginning to bloom this week. I've noticed spear pointed bloodroot piercing through leaf litter, and graceful, yellow trout lilies, with their mottled leaves resembling the color of brook trout. May-apples, also known as mandrake, carpeted shaded hillsides, with their nodding flowers poised between pairs of large deeply lobed leaves and on the verge of opening. I stopped to admire clusters of white anemone along wooded slopes.

The anemone is one of about 120 species of flowering plants from the buttercup family, the Ranunculaceae. Wood anemone have only one flower with 5 petals per plant, and are sometimes confused with rue anemone, which have distinctive, three-lobed, mitten-shaped leaves, and may have several flowers per plant with as many as six to nine petals per flower.

"Anemone" is derived from "anemos," the Greek word for "wind." Pliny said that the flowers open easily when the wind blows, and Theocritus said that its flowers fall and easily fly off in the wind. This may be why it is also called the windflower.

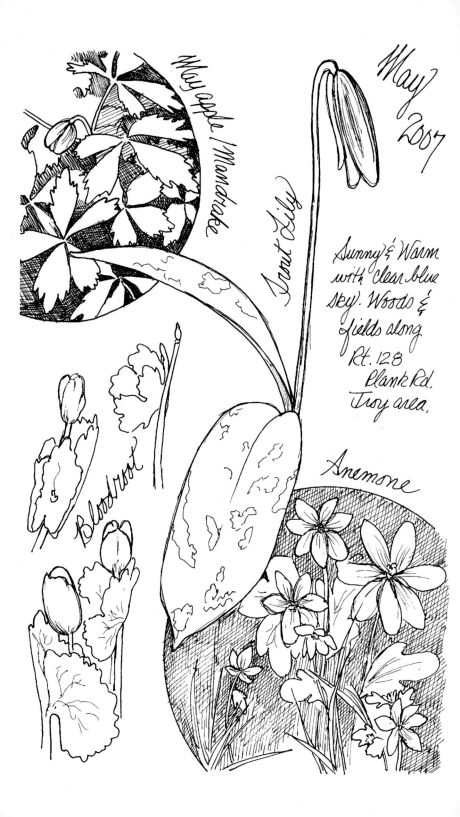

May 2007

Mayapple / Mandrake

Trout Lily

Sunny & Warm
with clean blue
sky. Woods &
fields along
Rt. 128
Plank Rd.
Troy area.

Bloodroot

Anemone

Ajuga Bugle Flower

Although wildflowers and herbs are often regarded as invasive weeds, I enjoy them for their own innate beauty, and often wonder what value or purpose they may have that we are as yet ignorant of. This week, amongst the blue-purple lilacs, periwinkle, creeping ground ivy and violets blooming, I noticed ajuga replens, or bugle flower, spread in large mats of color in my yard.

This perennial member of the mint family flowers from April through July. Within whorls, each miniature flower is oddly shaped, with a nearly non-existent upper lip, and a lower three-cleft petal that sticks out like a large tongue. Perhaps this adaptation aids bee pollination. Stamens protrude outward from the flower, and there is no scent.

The name "bugle" may be derived from the flower's resemblance to a thin tubular bead sometimes used in embroidery, and "ajuga" may be derived from the Latin word "abigo," which means to "drive away" or "banish." This plant was once thought to possess great curative powers to drive away disease and evil spirits.

Ground Ivy

Violets

Ajuga or Bugle

flower

Periwinkle

Lilacs

May
2007
Cold nights.
Warm, sunny days.
Many purple-blue blooms.

Turkey Vulture

Turkey vultures are primarily scavengers that feed on the remains of dead and decaying animals. They are very well adapted to this task.

With a heightened sense of smell and acute vision, vultures can easily find their next meal along a road, field or under the cover of forest and underbrush. Their digestive systems have special enzymes and bacteria that allow them to safely eat contaminated or rancid meat. As they pick food out from deep inside of carcass cavities, their bare, featherless, bright red heads remain clean, and their wide open nostrils allow them to breath while doing so.

Turkey vultures have long been misunderstood and maligned. Despite their gruesome diet and unattractive appearance, they serve an important natural function by keeping the environment clean of waste. They are actually non-aggressive and social creatures. To look up and see this large bird soaring overhead, its six-foot wingspan gently rocking side to side in the upward lift of a thermal draft, is quite an awesome and graceful sight to behold.

Spotted a large, charcoal colored bird perched in hunchback fashion on a barn located off Wright Road in Delmar, N.Y. Graceful in flight.

Too large to be a hawk. Not the right shape or markings to be an eagle. Noted small head and red face.

May 2007
Turkey Vulture

Carpenter Bee

I recently spotted some very large bees hovering and darting about the wooden eaves of a pavilion on fairgrounds where I was attending a music festival. At first, I thought they were bumblebees, but their shiny, black abdomens and unusual behavior gave them away as carpenter bees, also known as woodcutters.

Carpenter bees are common in the northeast, nesting in dead trees, and in the exposed wood of building eaves, decks, and fences. Generally, they are not harmful to humans. Only females are capable of stinging, but won't unless their nest is aggressively threatened. Males cannot sting, and spend hours at a time preoccupied with flitting about the nest and chasing away other male carpenter bees.

Although carpenter bees are considered pests because they tunnel into structures, their damage is minimal, as the holes are shallow. Prevention is possible by painting or staining exposed wood. With the disappearance of bees becoming a serious environmental issue, all need to be valued and supported as much as possible for their important service as pollinators.

Butterfly Identification

I witnessed a butterfly while visiting friends the other day, but failed to make a rudimentary sketch, take notes or snap a quick photo, thinking I would recall it later. The next day, all anyone could remember was that it was large and yellow with black markings. A disappointing and frustrating realization for me once I sat down to do this column, for I could not identify it.

Curiosity and observation are at the heart of enjoying nature, but real excitement and joy comes with discovery. To say, "I saw a tree, a flower, or a bird," is one thing. But to know it by name, and understand more about it, is quite a more satisfying endeavor.

When you encounter the natural world, intentionally focus your attention on it, using of all your senses to perceive what is in front of you. Ask questions. Note details of shape, texture, color, pattern, sound, smell, spatial relationships and environment. Learn something of it, even if only its name. It will enrich your experience immensely.

June 2007
Warm & humid.
Some rain

Large yellow
butterfly)
with
black.

Monarch?
(can they be yellow?)

Were wing edges
wavy, smooth or
ruffled?

Tiger Swallowtail
(same tail?)

Were
markings
spotted or
striped or
veined (like
stained glass?

There was no tail.

No
other
details
remembered

Variegated
Fritillary?

American Goldfinch

American goldfinches migrate in small, compact flocks, residing near open fields, swamps, thickets and forest-edged habitats, feeding primarily on insects, seeds and thistle. They usually nest where thistle is nearby, as they use the down from its seed-pods to line their nests. Goldfinches are also known as "wild canaries."

Throughout most of the year, both genders of the species sport gray to dull olive-yellow feathers with well-defined black wings, tail and white wing-bars. Additionally, the male has a black forehead. But when courtship begins in early summer, later in the season than most other birds, the feathers of the male gold-finch turn a pure, bright yellow that is hard to miss. His singing and calling to announce a found nesting site, chase away rival males and attract a female mate is quite lovely.

Most birds produce some vocal sound. But song-birds like the goldfinches, with their specialized vocal abilities enabling them to string together a series of varying notes in successive and recognizable patterns, sound like music to my ears.

June 2007 Albany NY

Hearing a birdsong I've never noted
before in this neighborhood. Then saw
a flash of yellow wings, undulating
flight across my yard. Goldfinches
visit my wildflower garden.

Wonderful!

American Goldfinch (Wild Canary)

Mobbing

In early summer, many birds are busily involved in the prime activity of nesting, breeding and raising vulnerable fledglings. Look and listen, and you may observe a common bird phenomenon known as "mobbing."

Mobbing behavior is used by smaller birds to defend themselves and their offspring from predator birds, prowling cats, or even you! First, one or two birds discover a threat, call out a noisy alarm and chase after it. A loud chorus erupts as more birds join in, and an aerial display of swooping, dive-bombing and physical strikes against the predator ensues.

Mobbing can occur within one species of bird, or flocks of different species, all in pursuit of one threat they share in common. Crows, blackbirds and starlings frequently mob raptors like hawks, owls or eagles. Songbirds will mob blue jays and crows.

Normally, a large predator can quickly do away with one small attacker. But mobbing confuses, annoys and harasses the predator enough to divert its attention and drive it from the area. There is strength in numbers.

June 2007

Warm. Big cummulous clouds in a vivid blue sky.

I dash off a quick sketch from the passenger seat — en route from Woodstock (to Albany).

Red tailed hawk in tree along Thruway)

Mobbed →

Fireflies

Call them fireflies, lightning bugs or glowworms, those luminous nocturnal insects you have fond memories of catching as a child are actually members of the beetle family Lampyridae. Approximately 170 species inhabit the US. I saw my first of the season this week.

A firefly's abdomen is made up of specialized fatty cells called photocytes, which contain chemicals that interact and emit light when oxidized, giving off a greenish glow. In the larvae stage, this warns predators that they are distasteful to eat. In the mature stage, male fireflies use it to attract a mate. Fireflies are the only bioluminescent creatures able to flash their light with precise timing, with each species having its own specific pattern.

Firefly larvae eat snails, slugs and cutworms that can cause damage to gardens. Their light producing chemical, luciferase, has been synthesized to make glowsticks, and geneticists have injected it into disease-causing organisms to test and track the effectiveness of drug treatments. I'm happy just to enjoy their magical, fairy-like glow on a warm summer night.

Evening
June 2007

Soft
green
glow, fading
in and out
amongst
the fleabane
weeds →

Firefly

Helderberg Bats

The Helderberg escarpment rises 1300 feet high, and is known for its dramatic cliffs, stunning views and geological significance. Layers of shale, sandstone, and limestone contain some of the richest fossil-bearing formations in the world, and include water eroded rock landscapes and many caves. But did you know that it is home to eight species of bats? This includes the Indiana bat, which is not only on the US endangered species list, but rare worldwide.

Bats make up almost a quarter of all mammals. They are the only mammals able to fly. Most hibernate in caves during the winter, but during the summer they may reside under the bark of trees, or in the crevices of buildings or bridges. The common misconception is that bats attack people at night. What they are actually doing when you observe their swooping behavior is eating night-flying insects. Bats can eat up to 1,200 insects an hour, including moths, beetles, cutworms, leafhoppers and mosquitoes. They provide an important benefit for the environment, gardens and food crops.

July 2007 Thacher Park

Beautiful blue sky and
breezy all day. Watched the
shadows & colors change on the
Helderberg escarpment. Might
have seen a raven. Later,
bats swooping by moonlight.

Ebony Jewelwing Damselfly

What I thought was a very dark butterfly fluttering across my path, upon closer inspection turned out to be a damselfly. A male ebony jewelwing damselfly, to be exact, genus Calopteryx, meaning "beautiful wing."

These 2 inches long damselflies have strikingly iridescent greenish-blue bodies and jet-black wings. They can be found throughout the eastern part of the US during the summer months, usually hovering and landing among grasses and plants that grow near the edges of ponds and streams, and feeding on flying insects so small you can hardly see them.

Damselflies are closely related to dragonflies, and with their elongated body shape they look very much alike, but damselflies are smaller and more delicate. Damselflies also fold their wings together above their backs when at rest, while dragonflies keep their wings opened flat and horizontal.

New York State recently ended a long-term dragonfly and damselfly survey conducted to gather information and gain a better understanding as to how best to approach the conservation of these insects.

July 2007
South of Albany in
Selkirk, NY — hiking
stream habitat trails of the
Hollyhock Hollow Sanctuary
Ebony Jewelwing
Damselfly

Notes

Notes